WICCA

A Beginner's Guide to Pagan Witchcraft

Sebastian Berg

Table of Contents

Introduction

Wicca is the beginning of a beautiful journey between your soul and the world around you. This book explains the foundation of Wicca, the beliefs and practices associated with the religion, and helps a beginner begin practicing Pagan witchcraft safely. If you are curious about Wicca, whether or not you wish to practice it, this book holds only truths about the Wiccan path of witchcraft.

Wicca is a gentle way of life that includes balance with nature; it is not devil worship. Wiccans believe everything is connected and remind themselves to be present with nature and reverent of her gifts. Wicca has changed over time and is now more open to those who wish to practice it. While females are most noted as practitioners of Wicca and witchcraft, males are still a prominent part of this religion. It's true that some covens follow a matriarchal preference over today's patriarchal religions, but Wicca is meant to be a balance between masculine and feminine, and should not favor one over the other.

By the end of this book, you should have achieved:

- A basic understanding of the Pagan witch-craft known as Wicca.

- What holidays and rituals Wiccans cele-brate and why.

- Tips and tricks to take away on your Wic-can journey.

You picked up this book either because you are in-terested in Wicca and practicing witchcraft, or you have a loved one who is. It's important that you are open-minded and willing to listen to truth rather than believe the lies that are told about Wicca and witchcraft. This book is simple but informative. Your journey to enlightenment begins now; enjoy.

Chapter 1:

What Is Wicca

Wicca is a spiritual journey of self and nature; it is not devil worship or sacrificing to Pagan gods. If you are reading this, it is because you are curious about Wicca. Either you are personally interested, or you have a loved one who is. Curiosity is good because that means you value knowledge and truth. This book will open your eyes and lay many questions to rest. Wicca is not this evil cult meant to turn innocent souls into demons. It is a spiritual journey and one that anyone can take.

There are a lot of terms used interchangeably with Wicca, but do not let the fear of ignorance in this world sway you from a path that is calling you. Wiccans are ordinary people that do ordinary things like drink coffee and go to work each day.

We never make children into meals and brooms are used as tools not for flight.

Often the term witch or witchcraft is used. Yes, Wiccans consider themselves witches, whether male or female. Witchcraft on the other hand is not all inclusive. You see, while Wicca is more like a religion or spiritual path, witchcraft is the act of casting spells. Not all Wiccans practice witchcraft, and not all who practice witchcraft are Wiccan. For purposes of this book, we will discuss both because to me together they make a great combination on your spiritual journey. Just remember they are not interchangeable.

The term spell is used for the magic aspect of Wicca and witchcraft. Even something as simple as a prayer in other religions is in this category. There are no giant balls of fire being hurdled at your enemies such as is seen in video games or tv shows. Witchcraft is understanding the universal power that is all around us and working with it to attain enlightenment, and at times heart desires.

Begin your journey of discovery and enlightenment with an open mind. You cannot fully appreciate or understand Wicca with a mind closed to new ideas, or a belief that Wicca is evil and should be eradicated. You may decide by the end of these chapters that Wicca is not for you, but at least you will know that it is a good presence in this world nonetheless.

A Brief History of Wicca

Wicca has been around as a religion for thousands of years, some say even longer than Christianity. Whenever it came to be is not as important as where it has come to now. The biggest difference between Wicca of the past, and Wicca of the present is inclusiveness. Until Raymond Buckland and Scott Cunningham came along, you did not learn about Wicca unless your family descended from witches or you were invited. Now, Wicca is an open religion that accepts all new members as family (for the most part).

Who you worship and how you worship is also more open than it used to be. In ages past, a Coven worshiped a certain god(s) and goddess(es) based on the High Priestess's preference. Today you can worship whatever deity or deities you feel drawn toward. This may change personally with time. You might feel drawn to the Norse deities one year, and the Celtic deities the next. Your ancestry may include heavy Greek ties, so you might choose that. Whatever pantheon you choose (or don't) is up to what feels right for you.

Wicca is and has always been reverent of Nature itself, and the masculine and feminine aspects of all living things. As with all religions, everything stems from the original wise man: the shaman. In tribes, the shamans spoke with spirits and nature seeking divination and guidance for tribal leadership, wartime strategy, and even healing. They utilized herbs and fasting periods to create hallucinations to gain knowledge and deeper understanding. Today we seek similar knowledge but utilizing modified, safer techniques to get there.

What Wicca Is

Wicca is a spiritual journey for an individual. It is also unique to each person. For some, Wicca is a means to connect to the world around them. For others, Wicca is a path to magic and personal gain. Whatever your personal reasons for journeying down this path, may they grant you the wisdom and understanding you seek.

Wicca is first and foremost a connection with nature. Nature includes the living force within all of us, and the universe as a whole. In Wicca, we acknowledge that everything has a masculine and feminine side. This is represented somewhat in the worship of gods and goddesses. Is it a requirement to pick a deity or pantheon? Absolutely not. However, doing so can bring you closer to understanding yourself as well as the world you live in. Taking time to listen to the world around you, letting your bare feet touch the earth, and sitting without purpose in silence with nature are ways to practice Wicca.

Wiccans also believe in reincarnation. True, this is not unique to Wicca, for there are many religions that believe in reincarnation, but Wiccans believe we only reincarnate as humans. Wiccans strongly believe that after the body's death, the spirit crosses into the spiritual realm for a period of rest. Once rested, the spirit returns to the living for a new adventure. If a spirit feels it has fulfilled its purpose, it stays in the spirit realm until it feels called to inhabit a body again.

Some Wiccans believe in the Rule of Three, which basically states that whatever intention or energy you put out into the world is returned to you three-fold. Therefore when you do good things with positive energy, good things will return to you in abundance. When you do harmful things with negative intention, then they return to you with more ill intent. That's where the term karma comes in, and it is very much alive in the world of Wicca.

What Wicca Is Not

The biggest misnomer about Wicca is that it is devil worship. Satan does not exist in our religion. Satan is a product of Christianity used to create fear. Wicca deals with the energies of the universe as a whole. When embodied in representations of a god and goddess, we accept the male and female aspects of the living world giving no particular favoritism to one or the other. At the same time, there is no heaven or hell.

Wicca is also not magic or witchcraft, and witchcraft is not Wicca. Wicca is a religion. Magic is another term for witchcraft. All who practice witchcraft are not Wiccan just as all who are Wiccan do not practice witchcraft.

Witchcraft itself is not a force that you make do whatever you want. You do not conjure something out of nothing. Witchcraft is a gentle force that you mold, shape, and wish into an existence that hopefully fits the intended outcome. Magic is the universal energy around you being guided to do things that it could otherwise do on its own but you are manipulating.

The Wiccan Rede

There are many different phrases for the Wiccan Rede, also known as the witches rede, very much like the golden rule you may have heard of in school.

Do as you will as long as it harms none.

This means whatever form your spiritual path takes, as long as you are not causing harm to yourself or others, you may do so freely. However, this does not mean that you cannot protect yourself or those closest to you.

Something else to remember about Wicca and witchcraft as a Wiccan, everyone has free will. You should not cast magic intending to take free will from another person. In fact, when crafting spells for other people, it is considered common courtesy to ask for their permission.

Chapter 2:

Pagan Deities

The Wiccan religion reveres the male and female aspects of the universal energy of nature. It is not necessary to put a face or name to this during your daily practice or worship. The Goddess represents the cycle of life and is depicted as the maiden, the mother, and the crone. She represents the cycles of the moon: waxing, full, and waning. Her symbols are the cauldron or cup and the earth and sea. On the other hand, the God represents the sun, the lifegiver of the living world, as well as the sky and fire. He is depicted as the horned God. Together the God and Goddess represent the cycle of life, with life beginning and ending at the Goddess and being fruitful with the God.

For those who find it much easier to communicate with that universal energy as though it embodies one or more gods or goddesses, within this chapter you will find some of the key deities in the seemingly endless pantheon of Pagan gods. The following pages will discuss some of the most common pantheons for the beginner to get started. If you're more comfortable speaking to nobody in particular, you can ignore this chapter. I think you'll find one or two that resonate with you and make your spiritual journey more personal by choosing one.

Celtic deities are by far the most recognized when talking with other Wiccans. However, as the religion has evolved, many different pantheons have garnered equal recognition. For purposes of remaining brief, we will focus on some of the most common deities of the Celtic, Greek, Egyptian, and Norse pantheons. This is in no way an exhaustive list, but it gives you significant options from which to start your spiritual journey in reverence to nature.

Celtic

From as far back as has been documented, Wiccans have worshipped gods and goddesses from the Celtic pantheon. Many of the Sabbats specifically mention these gods and goddesses if not named after them. The following are some of the most well known names in the Celtic pantheon.

Brighid

Brighid is a red-haired Irish goddess of poetry and the dawn. She is known as a goddess of fire. She is one of the triple goddesses and represents the home and divination. She is most often revered during Imbolc, one of the sabbats, during the middle of winter. Her symbol is that of Brigid's Cross, woven from grass and hung above doorways. She has also been revered as a Christian saint. She is often called upon for healing and comfort of the ill. Brighid often takes on the aspect of the maiden in the maiden-mother-crone cycle, but she is also appropriate for the mother aspect as well. Call upon Brighid when you need healing, safety in the home, and are seeking guidance on similar issues.

Cailleach

Known by the names of the Veiled One and Queen of Winter, Cailleach is known as the hag. She often appears as a veiled old woman, someone with only one eye, pale-bluish skin, red teeth, and wears clothes adorned with skulls. She is the force behind winter storms and is neither good nor evil. She protects creatures during the cold winter months. It is said by some histories that Cailkeach ruled over winter and slept while Brighid ruled over summer. She represents the cycle of life and death, though most often depicted for death. She represents the aspect of the crone in the maiden-mother-crone cycle. She can also appear as a beautiful young woman to those who offer kindness. She represents the truth, so do not expect to lie to her.

Cernunnos

Known as the horned god, Cernunnos is the hunter and symbolizes the fertility of the earth. Modern neoplasms have given him the name Lord of the Wilds. He has power over predator and prey alike allowing beasts such as deer and wolves to commune together in harmony though they might be natural enemies in the wild. He is often depicted as a stag or a man wearing an antlered helm. He honors the return of the body to the earth and guides the spirit to the afterlife. Call upon Cernunnos to honor nature as well as for fertility for the body or crops.

Cerridwen

The goddess Cerridwen represents rebirth and change. She is blessed with poetic wisdom, inspiration, and the gift of prophetic sight. She is often depicted as the keeper of knowledge held within the confines of a cauldron in the Underworld, and much of her power comes from potions she crafts within the cauldron. In some histories she is seen as a white witch, which means that her magic is usually used for good. She represents the mother and crone in the maiden-mother-crone cycle. Her symbol is the white sow, which represents the fertility and strength of being a mother.

Lugh

Lugh is the Irish god of kings, justice, and leadership. He is honored on Lughnasadh or Lammas on August 1st in memory of his victory over the spirits of Tír na nÓg. He is a skilled craftsman and represents the harvest. He was also known as the god of oaths and presided over nobility and royalty. He was known to be a skilled fighter, though he does not represent war. He often used his skills in trickery to fool his opponents and win. You can honor Lugh with symbols of the harvest such as corn or grains.

Morrighan

Morrighan as an individual is called "The Phantom Queen." Most often depicted as the war goddess in the form of a raven and sometimes as three sisters of the same form. Morrighan is also a goddess of the land. She appeared before battlefields as a warrior queen and goddess of fate, offering prophecy and favor to both men and gods. Her multiple correspondences can have her seen as a triple goddess, honoring both life and death. Her complexities make her a favorite among Wiccans, especially females.

Rhiannon

Rhiannon is the goddess of the horse. She commands the power of sleep with a pair of magical birds that sing man asleep or awake. Her symbols are horses and horseshoes, birds, and the moon. Make offerings of hay or music to honor her.

Egyptian

Gods and goddesses of the Egyptians are fascinating. Because the Egyptians kept such vibrant records, there are many depictions of their deities upon the walls of their buried cities and tombs.

Osiris

As the king of gods, Osiris represents the earth and sky. He represents both the underworld and the harvest. Honor him with gifts of your own harvest including fruits, berries, and grains.

Anubis

In Egyptian lore, the jackal-headed god of death, Anubis, judges souls bound for the underworld. Anubis represents funerals, a time to venerate the living who have passed from this world and are traveling into the next. Call upon Anubis when honoring someone who has died.

Bast

The cat goddess was one of the most revered among the Egyptians, who held cats in high esteem as protectors of the underworld. Bast or Bastet is seen as a war goddess as well as a goddess of fertility and protection for mothers and children. Call upon Bast for you or loved ones suffering from infertility to aid in conception.

Isis

As the goddess of magic, Isis is important to Wiccans who follow the Egyptian pantheon. Because she used her magic in the matters of life and death, she can often be seen representing these. Her symbol is a lotus, and she represents the triple goddess. She is popular among female-centric or anti-patriarchal covens.

Ra

As the sun god, Ra represents light and the male aspect of magic: the Sun. Unlike other Egyptian gods, Ra is not only representative of the earth but also of the sky. He is celestial in nature and exists in the heavens. He embodies life and light. Call upon him in all rituals for his guidance is sure to grant you power.

Greek

The Greek pantheon is popular in Hollywood entertainment and stories. Almost everyone seems to know the story of Hercules. Wiccans call upon them to bestow blessings upon their magic.

Aphrodite

Aphrodite is the goddess of love, but she also has a darker side: vengeance. It may be more appropriate to connect Aphrodite to lust and fertility. Her symbols are the sea, shells, dolphins, swans, and of course the rose.

Ares

As the Greek god of war, Ares was a masterful warrior and purveyor of justice. He is also known to have a bit of a temper. Make offerings (not sacrificial) to Ares before you "go to war" so to speak with a difficult challenge.

Artemis

Artemis is the goddess of the hunt and childbirth. She is a protector of nature and the living, particularly the young and women. She is known to be a virgin and protective of her chastity. Her symbol is often the moon, she is beside it rather than a part of it.

Athena

As the goddess of wisdom and war, Athena aids those who seek to do heroic deeds. She is typically honored in the spring. Her symbol is her gift to the Greeks: an olive tree. Athena's connection to war is one of strategy rather than ferocity. Her victories do not come at great loss or bloodshed.

Gaia

The very embodiment of mother earth, Gaia represents the earth, sky, and sea. She is the creator of life and magic. Rituals or activities that honor the earth such as recycling or cleaning up refuse are the best ways to give honor to Gaia; do so on Earth Day.

Hades

Hades is the guardian of the underworld, but he does not represent death. He does, however, demand proper burial of the dead so that they might cross over to the underworld with more ease.

Hecate

Another popular goddess among Wiccans, Hecate represents magic and women. She is the mother in the maiden-mother-crone cycle. She is a protector of those who cannot protect themselves, and she represents vengeance. She is seen as a dark and powerful goddess and should be approached with great reverence for fear of incurring her wrath.

Pan

Though not typically heard of among Wiccans, Pan is gaining popularity these days among new witches. He is usually depicted with panpipes and represents sexuality. His symbols include forests, pastures, and the flute.

Zeus

Depicted as the god of the sky, Zeus is often seen with a lightning bolt as a weapon. He is known as the father of men as well as many other gods. In fact, he is the father of much based on his prowess. He represents man in the prime of life, and his symbol is the eagle.

Norse

Norse deities were revered by the Vikings many centuries ago, but they have made a comeback in modern Pagan religions, including Wicca.

Freyja

A goddess of abundance, fertility, and war, Freyja represents the strength in women as well as the earth and water. Most call upon Freyja for love or sexual issues, but she is also a protector.

Hel

Hel is the goddess of the underworld; she judges the souls who do not make it to Valhalla. She is both black and white, neither good nor evil.

Odin

Odin is the god of all gods and represents the frenzy of war. When considering an offering to Odin, or any of the Norse deities, never give more than you have.

Chapter 3:

Sabbats and Esbats

Wiccan holidays follow the sun and moon, but there are also correspondences with the more common Christian holidays. Not all holidays are by dates on a calendar, though dates are added for convenience, and Wiccans use the turning of the seasons and the night sky as guidance for their most sacred days. This cycle is called the wheel of the year, and Wiccans attune themselves to the rhythm of the earth.

Sabbats

Yule - December 21

Yule represents the winter solstice. It is on the shortest day of the year and celebrates the longest period without the sun. Yule represents the rebirth of the sun, and Wiccans light fires or candles in honor of the day.

Imbolc - February 2

Imbolc represents the fertilization of the earth and the coming of spring. This is the festival of light and is represented by the element of fire. It is also known as Brighid's day, one of the Celtic goddesses. For Wiccans who wish to join a coven, Imbolc is typically the time of year that initiations take place. For solitary Wiccans, you can use this Sabbat to celebrate your own self-dedication to your spiritual journey.

Ostara - March 21

Ostara represents the spring equinox and is also known as Eostra's Day. This is the first day of spring. The light of day and darkness of night are in balance on this day. This day represents a time of beginning or setting actions into motion.

Beltane - April 30

Beltane, also known as May Day, is a day celebrated for sexuality and fertility. Decorating a May pole is common during this celebration as is the cauldron. Flowers are an appropriate symbol of this holiday.

Midsummer - June 21

Midsummer represents the summer solstice, also known as Litha, when the Sun is at its highest and the light of day is the longest. Symbols of this day are sun and flame. Magic of any kind is celebrated on this day.

Lughnasadh - August 1

Lughnasadh, also known as Lammas, is the date of the first harvest. Meals made from the fruits (both literally and figuratively) of the first harvest are common during this festival.

Mabon - September 21

Mabon signals the autumn equinox and is the final day of harvest. The light of day and darkness of night are in balance once again. The world begins to slow down for a time of rest.

Samhain - October 31

Samhain is possibly the most well known of all Sabbats. It is also known as All Hallows Eve and is celebrated with Halloween. It is a time of contemplation of the year that has passed. During this time of year, the veil between the mortal world (the one we live in) and the spiritual world (the land where our spirits go to rest) is the thinnest. This is a time of remembrance of those who have gone before us, whether celebration of ancestors long gone or family members who have only just left us. It is not a celebration of death but of the lives that were and still are lived.

Esbats

These events do not happen on specific dates of the year but rather every 29 or so days. While not technically considered holidays, esbats are a time for the working of magic and contemplation for Wiccans. Typically falling on one of 13 full moons of the year, rituals and powerful witchcraft are worked on these days. The waxing moon represents the maiden aspect of the triple goddess, the full moon the mother, and the waning moon the crone. Most Wiccans will use the power of the moon for their magical rituals due to the representation of the goddess, and also the taboo in place in modern times. It is much easier to practice magic in the dark under the light of the moon rather than in the bright sun of midday.

The full moon is used most often for its offering of power due to its fullness. Most Wiccans revere the full moon. The new moon is used during times of new beginnings. It is not as popular a time for magic and ritual workings, especially with the time demands of today, but the new moon is no less powerful for your spiritual journey. Even still, some Wiccans will utilize the growing power of the waxing moon and the fading power of the waning moon for other rituals.

Moons by Month

January - Wolf Moon

Use the full moon of January for spells on new beginnings.

February - Red Moon

February's full moon is good for purifying, dedicating yourself to your studies (spiritual or otherwise), and meeting challenges head on.

March - Plow Moon

The full moon of March is best for spells that involve success and hope.

April - Planting Moon

Spells for planting or fertility are best done during the full moon of April.

May - Flower Moon

The full moon of May is great for spells of good health, good luck in love, and for wisdom and guidance on either.

June - Strawberry Moon

June's full moon follows the May one with recommendations for spells on romance.

July - Hay Moon

The best spells for the full moon of July are for enchantment, health, success, and strength.

August - Harvest Moon

August's full moon is perfect for spells that deal with abundance, growth of plants, and marriage.

September - Wine Moon

Spells for protection, prosperity, and abundance are recommended under the September full moon.

October - Blood Moon

The full moon of October is often used for spell-work involving new goals, protection spells, general spirituality, and time when resolution is needed.

November - Dark Moon

November's full moon is a time for family, friends, and when seeking divination.

December - Cold Moon

Hope and healing are best done during the light of the full moon of December.

Moon Phases

New Moon

When the light of the moon is not visible on a clear night, you'll know you're looking at a new moon. If you live in the country, you can actually see the outline of the moon, and the moon appears black.

Use the power of the new moon for spells or rituals that involve healing, a time of rest, and banishments of negative energy.

Waxing Moon

The next phase of the moon lasts from the new moon to the full moon. This is the best time to draw things to you that you want, begin something new, and grow as a person.

Full Moon

When the light of the moon is at its fullest and lights up the night sky, you're seeing the full moon in all her bright glory. This is the most powerful phase of the moon. It is recommended that you practice your most important and powerful spells during this moon. This moon is also good for bringing forth positive energy and enhancing your psychic energy.

Waning Moon

The final phase of the moon leading up to the new moon once more is the waning moon. Energy begins to fade. Use this moon's energy to do spellwork to push things away from you such as negative energy or situations you no longer wish to be in.

Chapter 4:

The Elements and Other Correspondences

The key to spell work is how each part of nature reflects a certain element or feeling. Many practitioners of witchcraft will utilize colors, elements, oils, herbs, incense, stones, and many other things as correspondences for spellwork. In the face of simplicity, I recommend sticking to the basic elements, stones or crystals, and plants. This is neither an exhaustive or all inclusive list. It must also be noted that what feels right to you for a particular purpose may not fit what is written here; use what you find the way you feel it should be used. Your magical energy will know what to do.

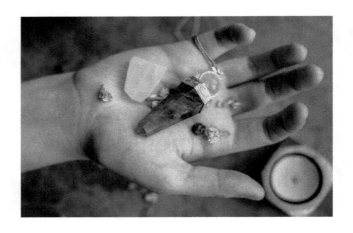

The Elements

Earth - North

Zodiac Signs: Taurus, Virgo, Capricorn

Colors: Black, brown, green, gold

Represents: Growth, nature, prosperity, money, manifestations, and material things

Air - East

Zodiac Signs: Gemini, Libra, Aquarius

Colors: White, yellow, lavender, light blue, gray

Represents: mind and psyche, wind, storms, purification, new beginnings

Water - West

Zodiac Signs: Cancer, Scorpio, Pisces

Colors: Blue, blue-green, gray, aquamarine, indigo, white

Represents: Emotions, intuition, subconscious and conscious mind, fertility, cleansing, ocean, lakes, springs

Fire - South

Zodiac Signs: Aries, Leo, Sagittarius

Colors: Red, orange, gold, white, peridot

Represents: Creativity, passion, healing, destruction, volcanoes, deserts, the Sun

The Spirit

The fifth element is the spirit, or self: you. It is at once all of the elements and none of the elements. It represents everything that you are and hope to be. The color represented by this element is the color that represents you. Maybe you're a water sign but you are really receptive to the color red, then your spirit color is red.

Stones

The number of stones and crystals and gems available for magical purposes is seemingly endless. I have compiled an effective but short list for your reference. You can find books on this subject that go into depth.

- Agate - protection, strength, courage, and love

- Amethyst - dreams, psychic energy, happiness, peace, and courage

- Aquamarine - peace, purification, psychic awareness, and self-expression

- Citrine - creativity, psychic powers, protection from nightmares

- Clear Quartz - an enhancing stone that magnifies other stones placed with it. A cleansing stone; place items upon it to clear away energies and purify.

- Garnet - strength, purification, protection, healing

- Lapis Lazuli - beauty, prosperity, healing, protection, joy, love

- Moonstone - grounding, divination, peace, protection, sleep

- Obsidian - protection, grounding, divination, powerful against negative energy

- Rose Quartz - happiness, love, peace, healing

- Smokey Quartz - healing, directs and absorbs energy

- Tiger's-Eye - courage, prosperity, protection, luck, honesty, divination

- Turquoise - prosperity, protection, luck, friendship, healing, happiness, emotional balance

Plants

There is an abundance of plants, herbs, spices, oils, and incenses that can be used for ritual spell-work. I have included several here for your reference and convenient use.

- Aspen (wood) - creating magical shields, protection, and healing

- Basil - happiness, money, peace

- Birch (wood) - banishing negativity, purification, fertility

- Carnation - magical energy, health, protection, strength, healing, love

- Cedar - healing, spirituality, breaking hexes, protection, purification, money

- Chamomile - sleep, medication, peace

- Cinnamon - love, success, power, psychic awareness, prosperity

- Dandelion - communing with spirits, divination

- Elm - feminine magic

- Eucalyptus - healing, purification, protection

- Gardenia - healing, peace, love, strengthening spiritual connections

- Honeysuckle - memory, healing, improving mental or psychic powers, weight loss, prosperity and money

- Iris - love, psychic awareness

- Jasmine - sleep and dreams, peace, spirituality, love, money

- Lavender - happiness, healing, peace, sleep, love, purification

- Lilac - purification, protection, beauty, love

- Marigold - protection, dreams, business, enhancing psychic powers

- Pine - protection, healing, money, banishing negative spirits, purification, enhancing energy of all types

- Rose - love, beauty, luck, protection, peace

- Sage - wisdom, prosperity, healing, banishing spirits

- Willow - divination, protection, healing, purification

Chapter 5:

Magic for Beginners

T his chapter will teach you how to craft basic spells and rituals. You will also learn the difference between a Book of Shadows, which you may have heard of, and a Grimoire, which you may not have. Wicca is a spiritual walk with nature and a way of life, but for some, witchcraft is as much a part of Wicca as the rest.

Book of Shadows

The Book of Shadows is probably one of the most well known pieces of Wicca and witchcraft. What is less known or understood about it is that the Book of Shadows is your journal of your personal spiritual experience. Anything that you do that pertains to your spiritual journey and magical practice belongs in this book. When you craft a spell, you write what you are casting the spell for, how you set it up, and what your outcome was over time. You also begin to build up a personal collection of how certain correspondences worked for you.

Every Book of Shadows is unique to its owner. You can create this out of anything: a leather-bound journal, a spiral-bound notebook, or even a private file on the computer. Whatever your method is, make sure to cherish it as a representation of where you started on your journey, and where you are now.

I recommend using the first page of the journal as a dedication to yourself and your craft. Talk to yourself about where you are now and where you'd like to see yourself in a year. Explain why it is that you have begun this journey and what you hope to gain from it. Date it. You'll come back to this over and over as a reminder at times of why you started and also how far you have come on this spiritual journey.

Grimoire

Less known and least understood is the book called a grimoire. I had not heard of this particular book until well within my own time with Wicca. Some, including myself before, mistakenly believe that the Book of Shadows holds all of the information you can use to cast magic and all of the knowledge about Wicca and witchcraft you know to date. However, the Book of Shadows is meant to be a journal. It's the Grimoire that holds within it all of the information you gather over time about shells, incense, and the many different stones.

Just like the Book of Shadows, you can create this out of anything. Most people customize their Book of Shadows to stand out with their personality. The Grimoire on the other hand is more like a compilation of everything you find along your journey. If you find a spell in someone else's book or online, you can jot it down in your Grimoire under a section where you save spells. If you meet or talk with a Wiccan who recommends something like a store or book, you can write that information here.

It is not necessary to keep two books. If you want your Book of Shadows to also be your Grimoire, go ahead. I do recommend that you use tabs of some kind to make information easier to find. I sort my Grimoire into different categories like deities, correspondences, and spells. I can add to a category or add a whole new category, but for the most part I work in only a few. I make the information easier to find for myself because this is my tool along the journey.

Magical Tools

Witchcraft is the process by which a Wiccan or witch directs the universal energy into a desired result. A witch does not need components or tools in order to perform his or her magic. However, because of the focus required to cast magic appropriately and safely, it is a lot easier for witches to utilize tools in their rituals and spell casting. The following are some of the most common tools used by witches for their magical work. I do want to reiterate that the magic comes from within and around the witch and not the tools themselves.

Altar

The altar is possibly the most important part of any witch's tool set. This is the spot where the magic takes place. Many Wiccans will set up their altar to be visible all of the time, similar to a shrine that has been dedicated to a god or goddess. The altar can be made out of anything. It can be a space on a table where you place a cloth you like and use only for special magical occasions. It could be an altar handcrafted out of wood. Whatever space you deem worthy of your practice is perfect, as long as you feel comfortable with where and what it is.

When setting up the altar for spell practice, there are many different schools of thought on where certain things should be placed. Some people have a candle to represent both the goddess and god as well as candles to represent the elements and cardinal directions. Others will have a single candle. Upon the altar are placed the tools and items that will be used in the ritual. I will list some of the most common tools used by Wiccans practicing witchcraft and explain what they are used for.

Broom

Unlike is shown in television and books, brooms are not a source of transportation for a witch. They are, however, a way to clean a space both physically and spiritually. You can sweep an area, even if you sweep only the air above a space, to clear out negative energy. A broom placed on the floor in the doorway of a home protects from harmful spells being cast upon the house or those who live within it. You can place one under your pillow to guard against bad dreams or nightmares. Wiccans sweep the area where the spell will be cast prior to setting up for the ritual. While doing so, you visualize spiritual cobwebs being dusted away to clear the air of any astral debris that might clog up your spell. It is common to gift, or be gifted, a new broom when you move into a new house. You can use it to cleanse your house before you begin to live there. Once a year, throw the broom away and replace it with a new one. This is done because over time the broom gets heavy with negative psychic and spiritual energy. It does not matter if you purchase or craft a broom nor what size it is. You can even use a branch from a favored tree; if you cut a branch, remember to thank the tree for its sacrifice.

Wand

The wand is an energy direction tool in witchcraft. You can draw the protective circle or symbols for use in rituals. This tool represents the element of air and the masculine energy of the god. A wand can be made out of anything that is fairly straight. You can use a stick of willow or oak or even a dowel rod from a home improvement store. Those with a creative spark may choose to create one. What you use is not where the power comes from. When you use the tool, it becomes an extension of your energy and is thus imbued with the properties you need it to be.

Cauldron

The cauldron is another one of those tools that is common to witches and witchcraft. Though we do not boil children or turn enemies into toads using one. The cauldron is a magnificent tool used to cook or brew magical foods and potions or even house the fire aspect of your spellwork. Those with an affinity for scrying can fill the cauldron with water for gazing. This tool represents the element of water and the feminine energy of the goddess. Anything can be used as a representation of a cauldron, but nothing is quite as satisfying as a legitimate iron cauldron. With all of the new age stores popping up, it should be fairly easy to get your hands on one. Mine has a three inch diameter and is perfect for my space.

Athame

The athame is a small knife that is used for direction of energy during spellwork rather than cutting. This knife is rarely sharp and usually has a black handle; black absorbs power. It has similar uses as the wand, but it represents the element of fire rather than air.

Bolline

As a cutting knife, the bolline is sharp. The hand of this knife is typically white. It is a more practical tool than spiritual one, but it is nonetheless useful.

Cup

The cup represents the chalice and is meant to hold a liquid of some kind. During rituals, a beverage created specifically for the magic is housed within. You can place water in the cup, which represents the goddess. The cup can be made of anything. My first cup was a small champagne glass I picked up at an antique store. It was perfect for my little altar. When you begin gathering your tools for your spellwork, you'll notice that things sort of find their way to you. That's the universe for you and a sign that you're on the right path.

Pentagram and Pentacle

Often used interchangeably, the pentagram and pentacle are actually two separate symbols. The pentagram is a five-pointed star that has been around for centuries. In fact, the Order of the

Eastern Star utilizes an upside down one to symbolize the biblical heroines in Christianity. It is not a symbol of the devil, which we already addressed as a Christian thing not a Wiccan thing. The five points each symbolize an element including the element of spirit.

The pentacle is a circle surrounding a pentagram and is a symbol of protection. It also represents the element of earth. Items intended for ritual cleansing can be placed upon the pentacle.

Bell

The bell is unique in that it uses sound vibrations for differing effects. These can be made of varying materials. As it is shaped like an upside down chalice, the bell symbolizes the feminine nature of the goddess. Ringing or striking the bell is used during or prior to ritual to ward off negative energy of spells and spirits. It is also a symbol of protection for the home and can be hung in doorways, on doorknobs, or placed on a shelf. For people who like to incorporate the physical environment into their rituals, the bell is rung to signify the beginning and the end of the spell. It is said that when you complete your spellwork, if you hear a sound such as a chime or ring of a bell that the spell worked.

Cleansing Tools

As you gather tools, you can do some simple spell-work to cleanse them of any energies associated with them so that they are blank slates for your own magical work. Cleansing should match the material you are working with. Sometimes this means holding the item under running water or burying it in the earth for several days to allow nature to draw out all energies within the item. Salt is considered an excellent purifier, though be mindful that the material is not adverse to it. My favorite method of cleansing is placing the tool or item onto a large quartz crystal. As quartz is a purifying stone, it works amazing at cleansing tools for ritual. The best way to cleanse quartz is to place it under the light of a full moon.

Candle Spells

My absolute favorite spells are cast using candles. These spells are extremely simple to prepare but also very effective. If you want a quick spell, you can use a birthday candle. I prefer candles that are big enough that I can carve my spell or outcome onto it. In fact, I will often craft a short poem for the spell. The idea is that the more time you spend preparing for it, the more energy you gather to cast the spell. Now, carving a spell into the candle does not mean you need to go learn some special alphabet or latin in order to cast magic. Whatever language you speak is going to be just as powerful, if not more so, than some strange language you are unfamiliar with.

As you hold the candle, carving your spell into it, imaging the outcome you are casting the spell for. With protection, I imagine sunlight and moon-light coming down and surrounding the person or object I wish to protect, cocooning them in uni-versal light. In healing spells, I imagine that same light entering the person, filling them with heal-ing light, and pushing out the bad stuff. In mon-ey spells, it is important to understand what you need the money for. You can imagine a bill being paid or a phone call saying "you're hired" if you're in the market for a new job.

When I'm done carving the words of my spell into the candle, I set it on a surface that will allow it to burn for the intended time. The larger the candle, the longer it will burn. For spells that are extremely life altering and important to you, I suggest big candles. The more time you spend working with this spell, the better your outcome will be. As I light the candle, I always welcome the element of fire to the spell. Once the candle is lit, speak the spell aloud. I choose to speak the spell three times because that is what feels right to me. If you only wish to speak the spell once, that is perfectly fine. Allow the candle to burn and carry your spell into the universe to begin working on it.

Never leave a burning candle unattended. And NEVER blow out the fire; this is seen as disrespectful to the element of fire and is taboo among witches and Wiccans alike.

I typically only allow my candle to burn about an hour. Sometimes I will let it burn while I am soaking in a bath. The larger the candle, the longer it will take, so you will want to repeat this daily including inviting the element of fire to the spell, speaking the words of the spell aloud, and allowing it to burn for as long as you can. At the end of the burning time, you want to snuff the fire out rather than blow it out. I do so by wetting my fingers and pinching it. You can get an actual candle snuffer if you would like.

When the candle has burned out completely, your spell has gained as much power as it can. Some people will not allow a candle to burn completely out. I let it burn out until the candle can no longer be lit again. I like to take the leftover wax from the candle and bury it in my yard. Some people do this, while others discard it. Either way, you have gathered the energies of the universe and wielded them toward your goal.

Now it is time to sit back and let the universe do its part. Write this spell into your Book of Shadows as well as the date you started and ended it and what you did with the remnants of the candle. Pay attention to happenings around you. Things that feel like part of your spell outcome, write those down. This could take weeks, months, or even a year or longer. As time passes, write down things that have happened that belong to that category of your spell: healing, protection, money, etc. Once you are certain you have achieved the outcome, even if it was not exactly what you thought you wanted, write that down too.

There are many correspondences out there, items that represent different aspects. You can choose colors, oils, stones, flowers, days of the week, moon cycle, and even time of the year to further influence your spell. Over time, you will decide what feels right to you. I like to get an essential oil and rub it on the candle, but I typically pick a scent that I enjoy. Remember, the power of the magic itself lives within you. Whatever feels right for your spell, do that. There is no set way.

Intention Spells

Intention spells are something new for me. Though if I'm being honest, they're not that much different than a candle spell. These spells are perfect for bringing about change in your life. Intention spells require a bit more work on your part. These are large spells that take time, so they are typically reserved for big changes in your life such as career, family, or even a home purchase.

Start with a notebook. Take this notebook or piece of paper with you everywhere you go. Think about the outcome you desire. Are you wanting to purchase the perfect house? Do you need a career change and don't know where to start? Write the basic want or need at the top of this piece of paper. Now write down what you really want or need this outcome to have with it. For a house purchase, what's the most important deal making or breaking things it must have or not have? This may include monthly payment, location, size, or even included land.

As you add your must haves and have nots to this list, you will begin to understand what is important and not so important for your intended outcome. Maybe you can't stand houses that are painted green or you want a small yard that is easy to take care of. These need to be on your piece of paper. You should spend at least one week compiling this page of information.

There are a couple of ways you can begin to release this spell into the universe to begin working. You may choose to get this paper out daily and read it aloud, imagining that your outcome has happened and you are living in that outcome currently. This follows along the lines of athletes who imagine that they have already won to give them the ability to win. You will do this daily as long as it takes to achieve the outcome.

My preferred way of releasing this spell is to use fire. My zodiac sign correlates with fire, and I feel an affinity for it. So I tend to use fire to cast all of my spells. That is probably why I enjoy candle magic so much, since it is a very basic fire spell. I make a copy of the intention spell word for word. Then I roll this up and place it into my cauldron. You could place it on a fire-safe plate or surface too. I call forth the element of fire and light the rolled up intention spell. As it burns, I read from the copy aloud. As I read each line of intention, I do so as though it has already come to pass: "I am living in a two story house on a 5-acre lot" or "I am working at a place I enjoy, doing what I love to do, bringing home enough money to pay the bills, and have some left over for enjoying life." Read through this entire list at least once. Again, my preference is three times.

If you have always felt an affinity toward a specific element, think of how you can include that element into your spellwork. Put water in your cauldron and soak the intention page. Bury the page in the ground or cut it up and release it in the wind. There are many ways that you can release this spell into the universe, even if all you do is read from the one page and imagine your preferred outcome has come to pass.

Write this intention spell into your Book of Shadows and journal what happens as time passes. If you are house searching, write down when you come across houses that fit much of your intention spell if not all. And when you finally reach your intended outcome, write that down too. When you return to your Book of Shadows, you will be able to see how you have evolved on your journey. This means that you will eventually have many Books of Shadows, and that's a good thing. Chronicling your journey is not only a nice way to go back and see how far you have come, but it is also a way to see what you have done for a spell that has worked the best.

Rituals

Rituals are the pieces of magic that most people think of when they hear Wicca or witchcraft. Covens long ago would come together and work these powerful magics. Rituals are used for more powerful magic and for celebrations during the holidays. Just because the word ritual sounds more involved does not mean that you are required to make something elaborate every time you wish to craft a ritual. Rituals do require a bit more effort and thought typically, though I have known some witches who can come up with a ritual on the fly. No way is more or less power, and you should prepare and perform this ritual the way that feels most natural to you.

For me, a ritual is all inclusive. So I spend quite a bit more time researching and preparing for a ritual, whether it is for a powerful spell or in celebration of a Sabbat or Esbat. The first thing I do is gather things that feel right and represent my intent of this ritual. If I am casting a ritual to cleanse and protect my home, I look for correspondences that deal with protection and purifying. I also find colors that resonate with me and scents that I like. If I am celebrating a Sabbat, I pick things that remind me of that holiday, certain foods, smells, and flowers end up on my altar for this event.

Once you have gathered everything you intend to represent your spell or celebration, the next thing you'll want to do is decide what you're going to say. I spend quite a bit of time doing this. Rituals are very involved. After all, you are opening your entire self up to the universe during a ritual. It's important to protect yourself as well as focus your spell or words of celebration. You also want to pick a time and place where you will be completely un-interrupted. This is very powerful magic, and you need your entire focus to be dedicated to whatever cause you are representing here.

I highly recommend a ritual bath prior to the rit-ual itself. If you prefer showers, these work just as well. As you bathe, imagine all of the negative energy and thoughts within and surrounding you are being washed away. Clear your mind of all thoughts and craft yourself into a blank slate. Imagine each muscle is relaxing and all tension is draining from your body. Use a soap you enjoy the smell of or one that you have chosen to represent your ritual.

Once you are clean, you may choose to dress in attire that you save only for spell work and rituals. This may be a special robe or gown. There are some that insist on being "skyclad" or naked. Unless you're very comfortable with yourself AND you live in the country away from prying eyes, you'll likely be like me and opt to clothe yourself. I dream of one day owning a special hooded robe for my rituals, but for now I wear clean jeans and a favorite shirt. Remember that this ritual is yours. Whatever feels right for you is right for your spellwork. Now is the perfect time to wear your Wiccan jewelry. Do you have something that represents your zodiac or that you resonate strongly with? Have you found the perfect pentagram or pentacle that you wish to wear? Rituals are perfect for this representation.

Before the ritual can begin, or perhaps as part of the beginning of the ritual, you will need to cleanse the space in which you are going to perform the ritual. If you are performing the ritual outside, this will not take as long as if you are performing it inside. If you have chosen a space inside, you will need to physically clean the space and then spiritually clean the space. Use a broom and imagine that you are sweeping away negative energy and unwelcome things from the space. Make sure the space you have chosen will offer no interruptions. If you live in town, it is difficult to avoid the sounds of the city when performing a ritual outside. Doing so at night will cut this down significantly, and it will lessen prying eyes as well. If you choose to perform this ritual under the light of the full moon, you'll have ample light for your spellwork. If you're performing the ritual inside, pick a room that you can be completely alone in. This is easier if you live alone, but even if you have a pet, you want them unable to interrupt the ritual. I recommend a room you can lock. Leave all electronics and sounds outside of the room and turned off, that is unless you're going to have some music for the occasion.

Now it is time to create a ritual space. If you have chosen to have an altar, place it where it feels comfortable for you. A ritual will create a circular barrier, so take that into account when you place the altar and where you plan to sit or stand for the ritual. Make sure you have plenty of space if you are going to use arm gestures or make larger movements. Place the tools and ritual items you want to use on the altar. There are so many examples out there of how to place things on your altar. I'm a firm believer in putting things where they feel right to you. I often align them in symmetrical or visually appealing ways to appease my obsessive compulsive tendencies. Some Wiccans are particular about what way you face, usually North, and where items fit on the altar. You could choose to have no altar and use your full body as the tool for your ritual; afterall, that's what magic is anyways.

Next, and probably the most important, is casting your circle. The goal of this circle is to create a sacred space where nothing untoward can enter it. If you focus your energies on nothing else, please spend your focus here. Creating a physical circle makes this process easier, so I recommend placing something around your space in the shape of a circle that keeps you in and other things out. I'm not saying fence yourself in, but even laying a string on the floor to surround your space is adequate.

Some Wiccans prefer flour or salt for this. Now using your finger or a wand or even an athame, feel the power within you swell and move out to the tip of the tool. Imagine that power hitting and creating the circular barrier. Draw the circle in your mind and imagine it glowing powerful and white with light. Now imagine that it forms a protective sphere at that barrier. This powerful globe of light and energy is enclosing and protecting your sacred space while you perform your ritual. Pour yourself into this.

Once you have protected your space, you may wish to invoke the rulers of the four quarters (directions) of the circle. Some Wiccans see them as guardians. You are inviting the ruler or guardian of the North or Earth to be present as you complete your ritual. Please be mindful while doing this step. If you are not careful, you can welcome spirits or entities who are not pleasant. If you are concerned about this step, write down how you intend to invite them within your ritual so that you are certain not to invite an undesirable entity into your sacred space.

Next is invocation. Call upon the god(s) and goddess(es) you have chosen to worship. Call upon the energies that live within yourself. I feel particularly drawn to the elements themselves rather than particular gods and goddesses, so I welcome them into my space to celebrate life with me. Imagine energy filling the space. If you're crafty, write a poem. Find a ritual online. Write words that feel right for the moment. Speak from the heart and just wing it. Whatever you do, do so with sincerity and with full devotion of yourself. Performing a ritual should feel like an extension of yourself and who you are. So unless you are a solemn person who must do everything by a book at all times, let yourself go and your energies will guide you for what is right.

If this is simply a celebration of a Sabbat or Esbat, sit in meditation and enjoy this moment of silence. Imagine cleansing yourself. Free yourself of all negative energies and open yourself to allow new and purer energies in. If you plan to do spellwork, now is the time to do so. You can even choose a candle or intention spell as above to work inside your ritual. Because rituals pool so much power, I recommend using them for your most important spellwork.

Next, take food and drink both as offering and sustenance during this ritual. Splash some wine into your cauldron and add some bread as offering to the gods and goddesses you welcomed to your ritual. Feed your body now that it has spent the energy in the ritual. I find that after a particularly powerful spell or ritual I am exhausted. Having a sort of snack within this sacred space allows you to replenish some of that energy so that you can complete the ritual. While doing so, imagine all of the power within the space slowly being grounded and returning to where it belongs. Thank the gods and goddesses or elements that you invited into your sacred space and release them to return to where they reside.

To close and complete the ritual, point your tool at the circle and imagine all of the energy you poured into the creation of it is being drawn back within yourself. I like to also breathe it back out into the world around me to allow a complete cycle of the power. Continue this until you can feel the power of the circle no longer. If you created a physical circle, now you will ritually uncreate it. Clean up the flour or salt, pick up the stones or cord, and return your space to its original state.

Always remember to thank any spirit or being that you welcomed into your ritual space for attending. Cleanse tools you have used as was discussed earlier in this chapter. You may very well feel physically exhausted, but you should also feel a sense of peace and accomplishment. I always feel sated once I've completed a ritual. Moving the energies within and around me in a ritual dance is very fulfilling spiritually.

Conclusion

F or many followers, Wicca is a lifestyle, and for others it is a religion. I think the term of religion feels sour to some because of the judgemental nature of some who practice more commercial religions. Wicca is no different. There are some witches who are judgmental of those who are not within their coven or dont practice their way. However, I am a firm believer in "do as you will, as long as it harms none."

There are those who practice Wicca and witchcraft for the power they hope to gain. To be honest though, this power lives within and around you. You don't make it bigger or smaller. You learn to use it, manipulate it gently into desired outcomes.

There are some who call themselves a green witch, a white witch, or a black witch. To be honest, I'm a believer in just being *a* witch. I practice the way it feels right to me. I adapt my magic and tools to my preferences. Some call this being an eclectic witch; I call it being practical. You do not have to be a witch to be Wiccan. If you wish to practice witchcraft and choose a type of witch you want to be, there are a ton of options out there. However, it doesn't change the fact that you are who you are and will always be.

I will take a moment to stress a couple of thoughts I have on the witchcraft aspect of Wicca.

Do not cast magic in extremes of emotion such as anger or grief. If your emotion is out of control, you will not be able to control your spell. Do not WISH bad things on people who have hurt you. I am a firm believer of the rule of three, but even if you are not, doing bad things to people taints the energy around you. You will become that which you sow. If you constantly react to situations with negative energy, your energy will stop being pure and you will corrupt yourself.

Do not cast spells on people, good or bad. I am a firm believer in free will. When you cast spells on people, you take that will away. If you cast a love spell on someone specific, you take away their free will. Who wants a lover who doesn't actually love them? Protective spells or spells of luck are safe. You are casting these on the energy and world around the person rather than on the person themselves. I feel that these are more acceptable, though I would still ask the person I am casting them on first.

Do not delve into magic you do not understand. Do not decide to try voodoo or black magic just because an actress playing a witch on TV does it. The energies and entities that you work with will be a direct result of your machinations. If you decide to call upon any spirit who will listen, you may very well welcome a dark entity into your life that begins to wreak havoc upon it. The world of magic is so sacred and beautiful, but it is also very dangerous if not treated with absolute respect.

I hope you have enjoyed this journey with me as much as I have enjoyed sharing it with you. As someone raised in a Christian home who has found religions of all kinds bitter to taste, I have found nothing but peace in my journey with Wicca. I have been doing this for over 15 years, and I still consider myself a novice. There is so much to learn. Never stop asking questions and seeking answers. It is such a healthy mindset to be curious.

A lot of people approach Wicca and witchcraft wondering where to start. I would consider everything you just read as a good start, but there's so much more for you out in the world. If you're a modern practitioner, seek out Wicca, witchcraft, and Pagan groups online. I will warn you that there are a ton of these and not all are created equal. If you find a forum or website that offers information without judgement, it's priceless. If you see discord and name calling, exit the screen.

The same goes for books. There is a huge market for Wicca and witchcraft related content. Some are generic fluff, and some are valuable. The problem is that it is hard to tell the good from the not-so-good. If you want my opinion, I would start with Raymond Buckland's *Complete Book of Witchcraft*, and Scott Cunningham's *Wicca: A Guide for the Solitary Practitioner*. These men opened up the secretive world of Wicca and began sharing it with the rest of the world. These are amazing places to start, but they should not be where your education ends.

I wish you the very best on your journey. Enjoy walks with nature. Discover gods and goddesses that speak to your heart. And if you feel drawn toward it, practice safe witchcraft and bring forth your dreams to fruition. This is the most wonderful journey of life. It has helped many get through tough tribulations, and it will continue to aid you through much more. Good luck and blessed be.

References

B. A., H., Facebook, F., & Twitter, T. (2018, April 22). Meet the Gods and Goddesses of Paganism. Learn Religions. https://www.learnreligions.com/pagan-gods-and-goddesses-2561985

Buckland, R. (2004). Buckland's complete book of witchcraft. Llewellyn Publications.

Colette, B. (2018). https://unsplash.com/photos/aC-GRIciHFck?utm_source=unsplash&utm_medium=referral&utm_content=creditShareLink

Cunningham, S., & Nightingale, K. (2017). Wicca : a guide for the solitary practitioner. Llewellyn Publications.

Edain McCoy. (2008, August 7). What Witches Do: The Esbats. Llewellyn Worldwide. https://www.llewellyn.com/journal/article/1722

Farrell, D. (2019). https://unsplash.com/photos/
Zo3-fb7EwPQ/info

Halila, H. (2019). https://unsplash.com/
photos/-AfRBlhuaHE?utm_source=un-
splash&utm_medium=referral&utm_con-
tent=creditShareLink

Kumar, G. (2017). https://unsplash.com/
photos/ve_uN9V8xqU?utm_source=un-
splash&utm_medium=referral&utm_con-
tent=creditShareLink

McCutcheon, S. (2018a). https://unsplash.com/
photos/FpTNWeYeRwc?utm_source=un-
splash&utm_medium=referral&utm_con-
tent=creditShareLink

McCutcheon, S. (2018b). https://unsplash.com/
photos/MhLjFJi3fRY/info

(1999). https://pixabay.com/photos/pagan-al-
tar-goddess-altar-wicca-1034856/

(2013). https://pixabay.com/vectors/penta-
gram-black-magic-pagan-152115/

(2014). https://pixabay.com/photos/stone-
henge-monument-prehistoric-2326750/